SUPER SCIENTISTS

THE
SILKWORM
MYSTERY
The Story of Louis Pasteur

PAT THOMSON

Illustrated by David Kearney

MACDONALD YOUNG BOOKS

Papa's Microscope

"Why does he *do* that?" Marie-Louise, known to everyone as Zizi, threw herself into the big leather armchair so hard, she bounced.

"Lower your voice, Zizi," said her mother.

"But why does he do it?" she repeated.

"It's embarrassing. As soon as we sit down,
Papa takes the bread and starts to pick things
out of it! He found a flour worm today.
Disgusting! In front of Monsieur Loir, too.
Sometimes, even *he* starts to do it too."

Zizi stopped as she heard her father's
voice. The door handle turned and Papa and
Monsieur Loir came in. She began to feel
rather nervous about her outburst. She
hoped he had not heard her.

"My dear," said her
mother, "Zizi is
complaining
about your
table
manners."

Louis Pasteur looked at his daughter.

"The bread, Papa," she said quickly. "I was wondering why you always pick it to pieces."

"I like to know what is there," he said. "I'll show you. Go into my study and get my microscope while I find some milk."

Monsieur Loir took the microscope and put it on a low table for her while her father put a drop of milk on a flat piece of glass.

"This milk is fresh," he said. "Look at it down the microscope."

Zizi squinted down the eyepiece. "Oh!" she said. "Everything is bigger. It's like looking inside the milk! And there are shapes in there. Lots of little round blobs."

"Now look at this. This is sour milk. Can you spot any difference?"

"There are different shapes as well," said Zizi. "More like rods."

"Well done!" said her father. He sounded pleased. "These rods are the living microbes inside the milk, feeding upon the milk sugar and changing it into lactic acid. That is what turns the milk sour."

"And your father," said Monsieur Loir, "by heating the liquid, has invented a process which will prevent those microbes souring your bowl of milk."

"Or your glass of wine, Monsieur," said Madame Pasteur. "It works for wine, too."

In time, the word pasteurization would be used to describe the method of heating food and liquid in order to destroy the bacteria that is harmful to people. But at that moment, Zizi only knew that her father had discovered something very useful and he had done it by looking down that microscope.

The Silkworms

Zizi opened her bedroom shutters. It had
been hot in the train from Paris but here the
air was warm but fresh. From the window
she could see terraces of mulberry trees on
the hillside. The family had come to the
south of France because the silkworms
were all dying and no one knew
why. Papa wanted to try
and find a cure.

"Anne," she asked, "how exactly do they get silk from worms?"

"I'll tell you about the silkworms," replied the maid, as she made the beds. "I used to work on a silkworm farm."

Zizi sat down on the window seat.

"It starts with the silkmoths," began Anne. "They lay the eggs which hatch into silkworms. The worms eat the mulberry leaves and grow until they begin to spin cocoons for themselves. It's those cocoons that we turn into silk."

Zizi looked astonished. "Does that mean Mama wears dresses made by worms?"

"Exactly. Clever little beasts, aren't they?"

"But why did you leave the silk farm? Didn't you like it there?"

Anne sighed. "It's the silkworm plague. The farms are all closing."

"Papa will help," said Zizi confidently. "He thinks he might be able to look through the microscope and find what causes the plague."

Everyone
worked hard
through that summer: Zizi and
her mother, her father and his assistants.
With Madame Pasteur, Zizi collected
mulberry leaves and arranged the baskets of
silkworms in tiers. At each stage of their
lives, they examined the silkworms through
the microscope.

Zizi soon noticed that the worms which
were feeding badly were covered in little
black spots.

"Look, Papa," she said, "just like pepper."

"That's what people call it here," he answered. "The *pébrine*. It means pepper disease." He took the dead worm, crushed it and mixed it with a little water. He put a drop under the microscope.

"Now look," he said.

Zizi peered down the microscope, adjusting it as she had been taught.

"What are those little round shapes?" she asked. "They don't seem to belong."

"Exactly! I think that is the disease. Do you remember the microbes in the milk? These round shapes are also microbes, different ones, which are living off the worm and killing it. Microbes are alive, you see. They can grow and spread."

"What must we do?"

"First of all, every worm, egg and moth must be examined carefully. We must find the healthy silkworms and use them to breed. Then, next season, they should be free of this terrible disease."

It seemed that they had found the answer because the first worms from healthy eggs did well. But then things started to go wrong.

"Papa," shouted Zizi one morning. "Quickly, look! The worms are dying." She gazed, horrified, at the soft black rotting worms.

As Pasteur examined the creatures carefully, Zizi looked at her father. With a little shock, she saw that he, too, seemed unwell. He looked so tired.

"Won't you rest, Papa?" she asked, nervously.

"No, no. I must find out why this is happening!" And he began to work harder than ever.

Then
one evening,
he came in late and
sat heavily in a chair.

"We have been wasting our
time," he said. "We found the *pébrine*
microbes but we did not look closely
enough. I found something else under the
microscope. There is a second, equally
deadly disease."

A Terrible Interruption

Zizi sat behind her father's big chair. She heard him breathing quietly. She was wishing so hard that he would get better.

It had been horrible. They had returned to Paris so that Papa could attend to his other work. One night he had come home shivering and complaining of a pain in his side.

That night had been the most frightening of her life. Everyone thought Papa would die. He could not move or speak. Mama had told her that her father had suffered a stroke.

Now, only a few days later, Zizi felt there was real hope. At first Papa had wanted to sit up. The next day he sat in a chair. Then he started to speak again and just now he had sent for his assistant! She sat, mouse-quiet, and the assistant came in.

"The silkworms," her father was saying, "I have been thinking about them."

"My dear sir, are you strong enough yet?" Zizi heard a little snort from her father. "I think I know how the *pébrine* spreads. The baskets are stacked above each other. All the material from the silkworms above is simply falling on those below. If the worms above have the *pébrine*, those below get it. I believe disease is infectious. It can spread from one living thing to another. If we are to prevent this, the whole area must be kept clean."

In the days when hospitals were as dirty as the streets, this was a new thought.

"What about the second disease, Professor?" asked the assistant.

"Yes." Pasteur thought about what he had seen under the microscope. "As well as the *pébrine* microbes, which were round, I saw something different."

"I saw it, too, Papa!" Zizi forgot she was hiding and crawled out.

"You here?" smiled her father. "So what did you see, little microscope expert?"

"Black marks. Like threads."

"Quite right." Pasteur turned to his assistant. "They were in the stomach of the moth, not in the worm. We must find a way of discovering which moths carry this second disease."

"And only the microscope will tell you that," said Zizi triumphantly.

The second disease was called the *flacherie* and Pasteur worked out a simple method of beating both it and the *pébrine*. Every moth laid its eggs on a separate square of cloth. A moth dies after laying eggs, but the bodies were kept, pinned in a corner of the same cloth. Under the microscope, they were closely examined for microbes, either the *pébrine* globules or the black threads of the *flacherie*. If either were present, the eggs were destroyed. In that way, only healthy eggs free from disease would hatch.

All that remained now was to convince
the silk farmers. They were very suspicious
of Louis Pasteur. A man from Paris! What
could *he* know about silkworms?

Zizi's Microscope

Once more, the
family travelled
south. In the train,
Pasteur lay on
cushions and Zizi
and her mother
worried about him.
He was working on
yeasts and wine as
well as silk and
cholera. Just as he
had discovered that
microbes soured

milk and wine, and caused disease in
silkworms, he was sure that microbes were
involved in cholera, a disease which affected
humans. He had always been used to
writing, researching and teaching. How
could a man who worked so hard ever get
enough rest to get better?

They were on their way to the Villa Vicente, lent to them by the Emperor. It had an old silkworm factory in the grounds, now abandoned because of the terrible silkworm "plague".

In the peace and quiet of the country, Pasteur began to recover, watched over by Zizi.

"Papa," said Zizi, taking away his pencil, "stop working and tell me how you are going to make everyone understand your work."

"Ah!" said Pasteur, his face alive again, "we have set up an experiment. I have sent samples of the silkworm eggs to the Silk Commission in Lyons. I have predicted exactly which will die and which will live. I must persuade the farmers to do what I say, Zizi, and you can help me. This is what we will do."

Zizi leaned forward and listened. She and her father began to hatch a plot.

But the eggs had to hatch first and Zizi was impatient. All the village waited with her, for Pasteur had given twenty-five sets of eggs to the workers on the Villa estate. He was raising twenty-five sets himself.

Then good news came from the Silkworm Commission. "Professor Pasteur has been proved right in every detail. All four samples behaved exactly as he had predicted.

31

Clearly his method of detecting the disease works."

Better still, there was complete success at the Villa. For the first time in ten years, the silkworms were back and they were healthy!

Several days later, Zizi sat at the back of a large room, wearing her best dress. Her father was at the front, his microscope on the table. The room was full of men. She felt very nervous as she looked anxiously at the mayor. He seemed to be their only friend in that crowd of unfriendly faces.

"Gentlemen," began the mayor, "our good friend Pasteur has something of importance to tell us about his studies of the silkworm disease."

Several people began to jeer.

There was a pause and the mayor shouted quickly, "If you want to make money out of your silkworms again, you'd better listen."

In the silence that followed, Pasteur explained simply his work on the diseases.

He told them that, by using a microscope, he had found the microbes of the *pébrine* in the worms. In the same way he had found the *flacherie* disease in the moths. The solution was never to use the eggs from diseased silkworms or the disease would be passed on to the next generation.

A man stood up. "What must I do to keep my silkworms healthy?"

"You must keep your worms clean and separate from each other. Most importantly, you must look very carefully for disease, using a microscope."

At once there was uproar all over again. "A microscope?!" "We're not scientists!" Even the mayor looked troubled. "We are plain folk here. You cannot expect farmers to use microscopes."

Pasteur replied calmly. "Anyone can be trained to use a microscope. Zizi, please come here."

Zizi stood up very straight. Her knees felt wobbly but she managed to march up to where her father stood.

36

"This is my daughter," said Pasteur.
"She will now show you how easy it is to use
a microscope."

When Zizi went home in the carriage that
night, she was still full of excitement.
"Well done, my dear," said Papa.

"Is it finished now?" she asked.

"We never finish learning," he replied,
leaning back in his seat. "I am making a kind
of journey. I've looked at living yeasts in
wine and living microbes in insects. What
about human beings? Microbes, germs –
they must play a part in human disease.
I want to understand these microbes, then
maybe we can prevent the disease. What do
you think we learned from the little worms?"

Zizi thought carefully.

"That disease can spread if everything is not clean." Her father nodded.

"That the worms could catch the disease from their parents."

"Yes," agreed her father, "passed down through the generations. And also that there is incubation. This means that a disease can remain hidden for a time but then break out."

"You have forgotten my favourite thing," said Zizi, sleepily. "The microscope. Without that, the silkworm mystery would never have been solved."

Epilogue

Louis Pasteur did go on to make important discoveries about human disease. His idea that microbes which cause infections could spread, whether by contact or by being in the air, led to safer operations. All over Europe, doctors began to make their hospitals cleaner, and fewer people died from infections.

With the same painstaking detective work he had used on the silkworm diseases, he discovered how humans caught a disease called anthrax. His treatment of rabies had dramatic results. People who had been bitten by animals infected with rabies nearly always died. Pasteur developed a vaccine which could be used against it.

Pasteurization, using heat to kill harmful microbes, had already become a new word in the language. However, of all his successes, the one which must have especially pleased Louis was the foundation of the Pasteur Institute, in Paris, where his work is continued by the men and women who carry out research, still fighting disease.

Timeline

Louis Pasteur was born in Dole, France on 27 December 1822.

1843   Studies chemistry at the École Normale Supérieure, Paris, an important teacher training college.

1847   Awarded Doctor of Science degree.

1849   Becomes Professor of Chemistry at Strasbourg University.
Marries Marie Laurent.

1853   Awarded the Legion d'Honneur.

1854   Becomes Professor of Chemistry and Dean of Sciences, Lille University.

1855   Begins studies on fermentation which lead to his work on wine and beer.

1857   Becomes Director of Scientific Studies at the École Normale Supérieure, Paris.

1858   Marie-Louise, known as Zizi, is born.

1861   Discovers that there are microbes in the air.

1862	Elected to the Academy of Sciences.
1863	Studies wine. Becomes Professor of Geology, Physics and Chemistry, École des Beaux Arts, Paris.
1865	Studies pasteurization and the silkworm disease.
1867	Becomes Professor of Chemistry at the Sorbonne.
1868	Suffers a stroke.
1878	Studies major infections: gangrene, septicaemia, childbirth fever.
1879	Studies chicken cholera which leads to vaccination against disease.
1885	Successful vaccination against rabies.
1888	The Pasteur Institute opens in Paris.
1892	Pasteur is honoured by the Sorbonne on his 70th birthday.
1894	The Pasteur Institute develops a vaccination for diptheria.

Louis Pasteur died on 28 September, 1895. He was 72 years old.

Glossary

bacteria These are tiny life forms. They are a type of microbe.

cocoons A case the insect makes to protect itself in its chrysalis stage – the stage between worm and moth. Silkworms' cocoons are spun from silk.

fermentation A chemical change caused by a microbe. When wine ferments, sugars are changed into alcohol.

incubation The period when the disease is developing but not showing itself.

infectious If a disease is able to spread from animal to animal or person to person.

lactic acid The acid found in sour milk.

microbes Very tiny life forms which can only be seen through a microscope.

microscope An instrument which makes objects look much, much bigger.

pasteurization A method of preventing food and drink from going bad, by heating it to kill certain microbes.

rabies A painful, dangerous disease passed on to humans by the bite of an infected animal.

vaccination A mild dose of a disease which, when given to people or animals, can stop them from getting the disease.